DERRYDALE BOOKS
New York

This 1984 edition is published by Derrydale Books,
distributed by Crown Publishers Inc.
© Peter Haddock Ltd, Bridlington, U.K.
Printed in Hungary

ISBN 0-517-43879-8
HGFEDCBA

The Fancy Dress Party
COUNTING BOOK

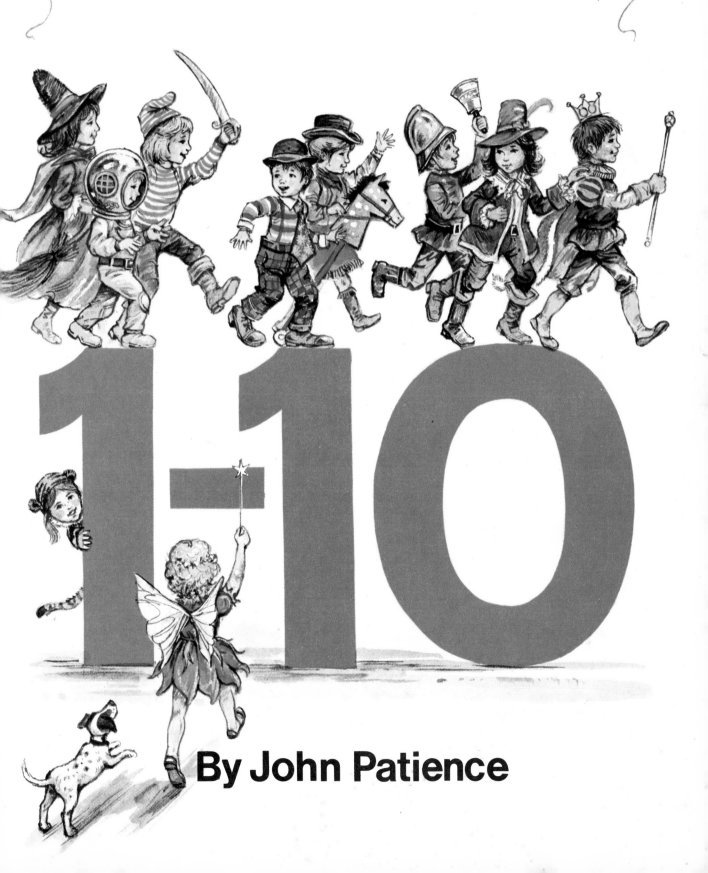

By John Patience

1.

One little girl was getting ready for her birthday party. It was to be a fancy dress party and she had decided to dress up as a fairy. Lots of other children came to the party. There were ...

2

Two
capering clowns

3

Three
merry musketeers

4

Four
crazy cowboys

5

Five
wicked witches

6 Six
deep sea divers

7

Seven
terrible tigers

Eight
fearless firemen

9

Nine
plundering pirates

10

Ten
royal rulers

This is some of the food for the party.
How many gelatin desserts are there?

How many candles are there on the cake?

How many glasses of orange juice are there?
How many glasses have straws in them?

How many doughnuts are there?

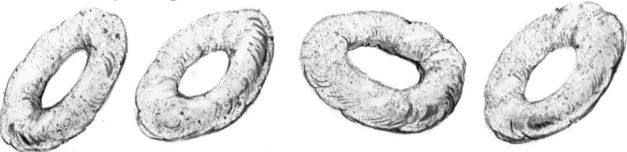

How many cupcakes are there?
How many cupcakes have cherries on top?

Here are some party balloons. How many are there?
How many red balloons are there?
How many blue balloons are there?
How many balloons have faces?

Here are some of the children at the party.
Can you count them?
Count the glasses of orange juice. Are there enough
for all the children to have one each?
How many balloons are there in the picture?